UFOs & A

Exceptional Cases

of

Alien Contact

By Eirik Leivsson

Table of Contents

Introduction 4

Chapter 1: The Flatwoods Monster, 1952 6

Chapter 2: The Kelly-Hopkinsville Encounter, 1955 15

Chapter 3: The Westall Encounter, 1966 24

Chapter 4: The Betty Andreasson Contact, 1967 31

Chapter 5: The Falcon Lake Landing, 1967 39

Chapter 6: The Pascagoula Incident, 1973 47

Chapter 7: The Medicine Bow Encounter, 1974 58

Chapter 8: The Allagash Abductions, 1976 67

Chapter 9: The Dechmont Woods Encounter, 1979 75

Chapter 10: The Rendlesham Forest Incident, 1980 81

Chapter 11: UFO Attack On the Knowles Family, 1988 91

Chapter 12: Peter Khoury's Intimate Encounter, 1992 99

Chapter 13: The Ariel School Mass Sighting, 1994 108

Conclusion 115

- © Copyright 2019 by Pine Peak Publishing AS -

The trademarks that are used are without any consent, and the publication of the trademark is without permission or backing by the trademark owner. All trademarks and brands within this book are for clarifying purposes only and are the owned by the owners themselves, not affiliated with this document.

Respective authors own all copyrights not held by the publisher.

In no way is it legal to reproduce, duplicate, or transmit any part of this document in either electronic means or in printed format. Recording of this publication is strictly prohibited and any storage of this document is not allowed unless with written permission from the publisher.

All rights reserved.

Introduction

We humans are naturally curious beings. Throughout history, we have continually been fascinated by that which we can't explain.

We have strived to gain more knowledge about the world around us, and to discover the truth about the nature of reality itself. Since the advent of the scientific method, our collective knowledge has expanded like never before.

There are certain phenomena, however, that seem to escape reason. Sometimes, all the puzzle pieces cannot be put together so easily.

Such is the case with strange enigmas like the Loch Ness Monster, Bigfoot, the Bermuda Triangle, and the existence and visitation of highly intelligent beings other than ourselves. The last mentioned is probably one of the most captivating mysteries of our time.

Many of us are fascinated with the idea of extraterrestrial intelligence. The existence of highly-evolved beings elsewhere in the universe is commonly thought of as probable. If any of them have visited our planet, however, is much more debated.

Still, people from all over the world have come forward with intriguing stories of alien contact — stories which seem to suggest that this may actually be the case.

While most of these accounts are compelling by their very nature, a few of them stand out as particularly awe-inspiring. Some of these exceptional, real-life cases are detailed in this book.

Chapter 1
The Flatwoods Monster, 1952

The Flatwoods Monster, also known as the Braxton County Monster, was named after the place where the strange creature was first seen. The initial sighting of this "Phantom of the Woods" happened on September 12, 1952 in the village of Flatwoods in West Virginia, United States.

That night, many people reported seeing strange objects hovering over parts of Virginia, Washington DC, and other places along the eastern part of the country.

13-year old Edward and his 12-year old brother Fred were playing football in the school playground along with their 10-year old friend Tommy Hyer. Out of nowhere, the boys suddenly saw a strange object appear in the sky.

They looked on as the UFO proceeded to crash-land atop a hill near the farm of their neighbor, G. Bailey Fisher. Startled, they rushed home to tell their mother, Kathleen May, what they saw.

Kathleen, the village beautician, grabbed a flashlight — as it was already 7:15 in the evening by then — and went with the boys to search for the object. They were now accompanied by three other boys: 10-year-old Ronnie Shaver, 14-year-old Neil Nunley, and 17-year-old Eugene Lemon — a West Virginia National Guardsman — who had his dog with him.

On their way to the farm, Gene's dog ran ahead and disappeared from their sight. They could still hear it barking, and was surprised to see it quickly running back to them, clearly terrified of something.

That didn't stop Kathleen and the boys from moving forward, however. When they eventually reached the top of the hill, which was around 1300 feet from where they started, they noticed a strange smell coming from an even stranger mist.

Kathleen described the scene as *"foggy, and there was a mist in the evening air"*. She went on to say *"the air had a metallic smell which burned our eyes and noses"*. After a few minutes, some of the group started feeling nauseated.

Suddenly, they saw what seemed to be a huge ball of fire, about 10 feet in diameter. It was a mere 100 yards away from them — but that wasn't all. A few moments later, Gene noticed a pair of small lights to the left of the fire ball.

He pointed his flashlight towards the oak tree where he saw the strange lights. Standing in front of them, they saw a tall figure somewhat resembling a man, but which at closer inspection was clearly not human.

For reasons unknown — possibly due to the mix of intense fear and the dark of night — the description of the creature varies slightly between the witnesses. The so-called "Flatwoods Monster" supposedly stood at around 7 feet tall. Some of them

said it was closer to 10 or even 11 feet in height.
Its diamond-shaped head was elongated, while its inhuman face was dark and had a subtle glow to it. Other witnesses described the creature's head as being hood shaped, much like an Ace of Spades, with a red, round face.

Its eyes were noticeably large and alien-looking. The body was completely dark and void of any distinct color. However, some of the observers claimed it was green, and that is was clothed from the waist down in what looked like drapes.

As the group froze in fear of the extraordinary and horrifying sight, the strange, towering creature emitted a high-pitched hissing sound before slowly approaching them. The alien being seemingly glided towards them, but then changed direction and went towards the red ball of fire instead. Terrified, the group ran away as fast as they could, without looking back.

When they returned home, Kathleen called Robert Carr, the local sheriff, and told him what had just transpired. She also called A. Lee Stewart Jr., the co-owner of the local newspaper "Braxton Democrat". Carr, along with his deputy Burnell Long, went to the Fisher farm to investigate the scene.

When the two men got there, they could still smell the pungent, nauseating scent. The sheriff described the scent as a *"sickening, burnt, metallic odor"*. Carr and Long combed the area separately, but found nothing else to prove the encounter. Meanwhile, Stewart conducted interviews with all of the witnesses. He would later venture to the location of the encounter together with Gene Lemon, who showed him around the scene and explained the details of the incident.

Come morning, Stewart went to the scene accompanied by one of Kathleen's sons and did some investigating of his own. He found two elongated tracks and some black liquid in the mud. Stewart speculated that it might have been the imprint of a UFO landing.

He made this assumption after discovering that no vehicle had passed through that area in over a year. However, it was later revealed that local Max Lockard, who got hold of the news, drove his 1942 Chevrolet pickup truck to the scene a few hours before Stewart went there.

It turned out that some of the boys called their classmates and told them what they witnessed. Lockard also heard about the sighting and got curious, and left several skid marks while he was there.

Many of those who claimed to have encountered the creature got sick shortly after the event. They all experienced nasal irritation and inflammation of the throat. Gene Lemon was vomiting and convulsing the following night, and developed throat problems which lasted for weeks.

Much to his sorrow, Gene's dog also became sick, and died a few weeks later from the illness. The witnesses believed that their exposure to the pungent mist that surrounded the area of the sighting had caused their condition. A doctor who examined them noted that they had the same symptoms as someone who had been exposed to mustard gas.

"UFOlogists" Gray Barker, Ivan T. Sanderson, and Major Donald E. Keyhoe did their own investigation of the incident, and firmly concluded that Kathleen and the boys did have an encounter of the third kind that night. They also believed that the illuminated objects seen nearby were connected to the appearance of the so-called Flatwoods Monster.

Of course, as with any paranormal event, there were outspoken skeptics. Sheriff Carr, Johnny Lockard, father of Max, and two US Air Force men who disguised themselves as reporters were very vocal that what everyone saw was merely a meteor. Carr also thought that the two lights that Gene Lemon saw that night merely belonged to some animal whose eyes reflected a light or shone through the dark.

The two disguised Air Force men also interviewed a local man who claimed he saw something fall from the sky. The man figured it was an aircraft about to crash land, so he promptly alerted the sheriff. In fact, Sheriff Carr and Long were about to head home from their investigation of this supposed crash (which came up empty) the same night Kathleen called them regarding the alien encounter.

Most non-believers consider the Flatwoods Monster as nothing more than a Tyto Alba —a kind of owl which somewhat resembles the description made by Kathleen and the boys. However, according to all of the eyewitness descriptions, this type of owl doesn't even come close to being the size of the alien creature.

Further investigation discovered that there were other people in the 20-mile radius from the Fisher farm who witnessed the bright-lit objects floating in the sky, around the time of the first sighting of the creature. One man from Birch River claimed he saw a shining, orange object steadily hovering in circles above the Flatwoods area.

A couple was also reported to have seen the creature, as well as the bright lights in the sky, while a woman and her mother — who were situated eleven miles from the scene of the encounter — saw a towering figure in the distance, which is believed to be the same, strange being. These are just a few of the staggering 116 reported sightings of UFOs and/or an unknown being during that eventful night.

The summer of 1952 would later be known as the "Summer of Saucers", as lots of UFO sightings were reported at the time. It is rumored that the US Air Force knew about the frequent displays of the apparent extraterrestrial visitors, and ordered their personnel to shoot them down.

One event that people connect with the sightings was the death of 2nd Lt. John A. Jones, Jr. and radar observer John Del Curto. The two were aboard a USAF F-94 fighter plane when they perished under mysterious circumstances. This happened on September 12, 1952.

Some officers, now retired, claimed that fighter jets were sent to intercept flying saucers that flew over Washington DC and the eastern part of the United States. Four of these UFOs reportedly received direct hits, and one in particular seemed to have crash landed in West Virginia — which is believed to be the craft that was connected to the Flatwoods Monster.

General Benjamin Chidlaw, then Head of Air Defense Command, was quoted as saying their unit had stacks of reports about the UFOs, and that they took them seriously because they *"lost many men and planes trying to intercept them."* If those words truly came out of a respected general's mouth, then the existence of UFOs, especially during that summer of 1952, shouldn't be so easily scoffed at.

Edward J. Ruppelt, Project Blue Book mainstay and the man who coined the term "unidentified flying object" (UFO), was also quoted as saying there were other, more serious *'duels of death'* taking place in the sky, which many believe pertain to high-speed chases, collisions or even aerial battles between man and ETs.

Chapter 2
The Kelly-Hopkinsville Encounter, 1955

On August 21, 1955, Billy Ray Taylor and his family from Pennsylvania were visiting Elmer "Lucky" Sutton and his family at their farmhouse in Kelly, a town near the city of Hopkinsville — located in the rural area of Christian County, Kentucky, USA.

As the Taylors and Suttons were spending the evening catching up inside the farmhouse, Billy Ray went outside to get some water from the water pump. Suddenly, he noticed a number of odd lights hovering in the western sky. Looking closely, he realized that there was a disc-shaped craft with different-colored lights illuminating the sides.

Standing there awe-struck for a moment, Billy Ray hastily ran back inside to alert the rest of the group. Elmer dismissed his wild claims with a cheeky smile, insisting that it was nothing but a shooting star. Not wanting to seem crazy, Billy Ray calmed down and took his seat at the family table.

An hour later, the Sutton's dog — who was outside in the yard

— started barking, and strange noises could be heard nearby. Suddenly, the barking stopped completely, and the dog was heard scrambling across the yard before it went completely quiet. It would later be discovered that the dog hid under the house and stayed there until the next morning, as a result of what greeted it near the Sutton's lawn.

Worried about the sudden silence from their trusted canine, Billy Ray and Elmer went outside, armed with shotguns and ready for action. As they peeked outside the main entrance, they were met with an astonishing sight. Standing near the front of the house was a stranger of a very different kind.

The witnesses would later describe the being as standing around 3 feet tall with a silver body — possibly a metallic suit. It had long arms with talon-like hands and thin, weak-looking legs. Its ears were especially pronounced, with a long and pointy look to them. At times the being appeared to be floating, and moved in a strange manner, as if it was wading through water.

As soon as creature and the two men spotted each other, the being started walking towards them with its hands raised up in the air. Though the creature seemed to be surrendering or — at least — did not seem to be hostile, the two men unloaded their guns on it out of pure terror.

Billy Ray and Elmer were quite experienced with their firearms, and were absolutely sure that they hit the creature — which stood a mere 20 feet from them. To their surprise, they clearly heard what sounded like bullets bouncing off a metal drum. Despite this violent hail of gunfire, however, the unknown creature simply turned around and headed towards the nearby woods at great speed.

Elmer and Billy Ray decided to chase after the creature, but even before they could leave the porch, they noticed a small hand reaching for them from the roof. They quickly shot at it, and down floated another, seemingly identical, creature to the ground, before scurrying away into some trees nearby and disappearing from sight.

The two men rushed inside the house in a near-panicked state and scrambled to lock the front door. J.C. Sutton — Elmer's brother — saw another creature peeking through one of the windows a few minutes later. They fired at it, breaking the window and leaving a number of holes on the screen.

Throughout the evening, the creatures kept coming back and peeking through the windows, as if they were taunting the terrified family. The group got the impression that there were around 12 to 15 of the creatures. However, they never saw more than 2 of them at the same time.

The creatures were now scampering on top of the roof as if they were trying to break into the farmhouse. The men of the family continued to frantically shoot at the windows and the walls, in a desperate attempt to get rid of the alien creatures. This went on for hours, before the family finally decided to rush out and get help.

At 11 in the evening, the two families hurried outside and managed to get to their vehicles. With adrenaline pumping, they drove directly to the Hopkinsville Police Station where they were led to Sheriff Russell Greenwell — the town's chief of police.

Greenwell got the impression that the group was scared *"beyond reason by something beyond their comprehension"*.

In fact, when Billy Taylor's pulse was checked, it was double that of the normal rate. He further described the Suttons as the kind who rarely asked for help from the authorities, and that they were sober and — as far as he could tell — completely sane.

Understandably, the police were initially highly skeptical of the family's story. When Greenwell and 20 other officers were finally convinced to go to the scene, however, they noticed the bullet holes that riddled the house, along with hundreds of empty bullet shells that were spread around.

Even so, there were no signs of the strange intruders. The police went around the neighborhood and discovered that other people, including police officers and a state highway trooper, witnessed strange lights and noises coming from the sky.

The highway trooper reported seeing meteor-like objects in the air that made a sound similar to artillery fire. The police tried to locate the source of the lights or any trace of the alien intruders, but to no avail. However, they did find a luminous patch on the fence where one of the creatures was supposedly shot.

The mysterious patch was photographed, but unfortunately a sample wasn't collected, which hindered any further, serious investigation of the inexplicable substance.

The authorities eventually left the neighborhood around 2:15 in the morning, with nothing to bring back to the station except various eyewitness accounts of unknown phenomena. Soon after they left the Sutton's farmhouse, however, the strange creatures eventually returned and peered through the windows once again. The family responded with a new barrage of frantic gunshots.

Since the families felt trapped and were unable to sleep, this went on until 4:35 in the morning, before the police were alerted once again. This time, they sought help from the Air Force. By this time, the creatures had long since disappeared, and Elmer and Billy Ray had momentarily left to take care of some important business. Representatives from the Air Force came to the scene, surveyed the area, and interviewed the rest of the family members one by one.

Naturally, the strange story quickly caught the attention of the local news media. The *Kentucky New Era* newspaper published the story of the alleged alien visitors, which was met with harsh ridicule by most of its readers. The families didn't want any publicity at all, and were highly upset when they knew the story had leaked to the press.

They did not receive any money from the media whatsoever. UFOlogists have later made note of this, adding that it made no sense for them to shoot up their own house, only to spend their hard-earned money to repair the damages and get ridiculed by their neighbors and fellow townsfolk.

Elmer, Billy Ray and five others from the group were later interviewed on live radio by Andrew "Bud" Ledwith — who happened to be an engineer and a professional artist. Ledwith drew what was later to be known as the "goblins" or "green men" of Hopkinsville. Oddly enough, with the combination of their seemingly-mischievous taunting and their particular appearance, the beings seem to draw many parallels to the creatures known as goblins from medieval folklore.

Most people saw this event as a hoax, but that didn't stop many interested parties from coming to see the place where the extraordinary encounter supposedly happened. Not wanting to become an attraction, the Suttons readily tried to get rid of these curious tourists. However, when it became clear that they couldn't keep the people from coming, they decided that charging them a fee would discourage most of them.

Though the family did earn some money after a while, they were not happy with what was occurring, so they finally refused everyone altogether — putting up signs and fences to repel newcomers. They were also adamant about not giving interviews from then on — turning down journalists, authors and UFO-enthusiasts alike.

Skeptics of the Hopkinsville encounter believe that what the people of the town saw that night were not UFOs or alien beings, and came up with a number of mundane — if somewhat unfounded — explanations. Major John E. Albert of the U.S. Air Force claimed that the supposed aliens were actually silver-painted monkeys that could have escaped from the circus.

Renaud Lecletit, a French UFOlogist, thought the strange beings were the nocturnal yellow-eyed great horned owls — though he failed to explain their highly-uncharacteristic behavior and seemingly-supernatural ability to avoid gunshots. Joe Nickell, a known skeptic of paranormal occurrences, believed that the sightings of lights in the sky were not UFOs, but simply meteors.

A year after the Kelly-Hopkinsville Encounter, Dr, Joseph Allen Hynek of the Center for UFO Studies — or CUFOS — managed to get a hold of two persons privy to detailed information about the encounter. Another UFO aficionado, Isabel Davis, also conducted her own investigation into the events.

The two, along with Ledwith (the engineer and radio host), agreed that what the Suttons and Taylors saw that night were indeed some sort of unknown beings. Since then, UFOlogists have considered the Hopkinsville Goblins case as one of the most notable examples of close encounters with intelligent, alien lifeforms.

Nowadays, the event that took place on that fateful night of August 21, 1955 has become an attraction of sorts, especially among the townsfolk of Kelly, Hopkinsville. In fact, the locals now celebrate the Kelly "Little Green Men" Days Festival every third weekend of August.

Chapter 3
The Westall Encounter, 1966

April 6, 1966, on a bright morning in Clayton — a suburb in Melbourne, Australia — one of the most notorious incidents in UFO history took place. It was a sunny, breezy morning, perfect for the students of Westall High School to partake in normal fitness activities and enjoy the wonderful outdoors.

It was just past 11 AM when a bizarre aircraft streaked across the sky. It loomed, massive and metallic, hovering above pine trees about a quarter mile behind the school. The children and their instructors watched in abject fascination as the dazzling, disc-like craft sat above the trees. It was unlike anything they'd ever seen before. It was truly a massive sight — about the size of two large cars.

Abruptly, the craft flew across the field behind the school and then returned to its position stationary above the pine trees, before descending out of sight — hidden behind the tree boughs. Swooping in from the opposite direction of the craft were what appeared to be four or five private aircrafts — darting after the object which then disappeared behind the pine trees.

Bursting into view, the gargantuan UFO rose to meet the private aircrafts and seemed to face off. In an elaborate game of cat and mouse, the foreign vessel took off and the other aircrafts followed in quick pursuit. They were no match for the speed of the silver disk. In a flash, it took off into the distance, and the jets finally gave up their pursuit. This whole ordeal took place in an estimated span of 20 minutes.

With over 200 witnesses and varying stories that increase in both strangeness and horror, the Westall UFO encounter is thought to be one of the biggest UFO/ET cover-ups in existence.

Considering all the witnesses and media coverage, it is astounding (and quite suspect) that there was so little information that came up in the years after the event. Decades after the incident, however, reports and testimonies finally began to surface. These shed new light on the encounter with the eerie silver object in the sky, and further perpetuated the notion that someone, or something, persuaded the witnesses to keep their silence.

Andrew Greenwood — a teacher at the high school and one of the few staff members said to have witnessed the disk — initially relayed his story to the local newspapers. Greenwood reported seeing the object flash above the pine trees in what looked like a stunning beam of light.

Later in his life, Greenwood revealed the he was eventually visited by men at his residence who told him to keep quiet, citing the Official Secrets Act of Australia. If he didn't, they would get him fired from the school, and discredit his statements by spreading rumors of him being an unstable alcoholic.

A student of Greenwood's who also saw the UFO, claimed that it was a huge silver craft that was hunted by a group of Cessna planes as it floated over the pine trees. When the craft rose to the height of the Cessna's, the student said it appeared to be of a similar length, only much thinner.

The student, along with two of his friends, decided to

investigate the field behind the pine trees where the craft descended for a few moments before the Cessnas arrived. They were met with a hefty, flattened circle that had no telling track marks near it. No ordinary animal or machinery seemed to have made it; it had to have come from above.

As if that was not alarming enough, additional reports of the incident tell of a girl who was found unconscious near the area where the craft hovered. Students confessed that the girl, a trained runner, dashed to the area and got there well before anyone else could.

After the silver craft took off, they were startled to find the girl collapsed and dazed. An ambulance was rushed to the scene and supposedly took the young girl to a hospital. In a spooky turn of events, the girl never returned to Westall High.

Stranger still, when a good friend of hers went to check on her, she was met with a woman who claimed that the girl never even lived there. The girl and her family were gone. Other witness accounts paint a vivid picture of two smaller, disk-like crafts that sat near the front of Westall High, but these testaments are scattered and few in number.

So how, with a witness head count of over 200, is it possible to have so many gaps in the story? UFO enthusiasts and conspiracy dabblers alike whisper of a cover-up, and there are indeed certain accounts that give off some red flags.

On April 9, 1966, the scene of the UFO-field behind the trees- was invaded by military personnel shortly after the incident. Truckloads of people scoured the area with devices that closely resembled metal detectors. The men were said to have taken precise measurements of the depression made by the craft and then burned the evidence.

Some skeptics claim that, although the military arrived, there was nothing found because there was no official report filed. They say that, had there been evidence, surely there would have been documentation.

In another account, the farmer who owned the land, sick of everyone trespassing to visit the site, admitted to burning the land himself. All in all, the details surrounding the authorities' operation in the area remain murky. But then again, most experienced UFO researchers would expect as much.

Just five days after the military left, the Dandenong Journal, a news source in the area, was told that staff and students from the school would not allow additional interviews, and denied any and all reporters from investigating.

It is rumored that two men in navy suits showed up to the school and advised the staff to steer clear of the media and to not speak a word about what they saw — there was nothing extraterrestrial going on, they insisted. Some testimonies even state that the head of the faculty was threatened by the men.

In a twist that seems to confirm the presence of these men, the headmaster called an emergency assembly where he proceeded to inform the students that the silver object was nothing but a balloon deployed by the military as part of a project, and that they should remain secretive about what happened. One teacher who had presence of mind to whip out her camera was allegedly taken roughly aside and forced to give up her film.

The final clue to the UFO event was a video made by a local news team. News Channel 9 GTV allegedly recorded witness accounts of the flying saucer, which they stored on tape and broadcasted a single time. That tape — which was placed in their archives where nothing had ever gone missing before — inexplicably disappeared.

Over the years, many experts and armchair skeptics have tried to debunk the Westall UFO encounter. Some note the school's close proximity to an airport, where they could have been testing secret military jets. However, during this time,

Australia was not much involved with developing new aircrafts, as they'd just barely recovered after the war. Those aircrafts that were produced around that period have since been declassified, which show that there weren't any military jets at that airport in 1966.

Others note that a large, silver weather balloon was allegedly launched some two hours before the incident, and could theoretically have been in the vicinity of Clayton during the incident. This, however, does not account for the disc shape, nor the sporadic, high-speed movements of the object.

To this day, UFO enthusiasts and skeptics alike are still trying to get to the bottom of this mystery.

Chapter 4
The Betty Andreasson Contact, 1967

On a chilly winter night in South Ashburnham, Massachusetts, on January 25, 1967, Betty Andreasson was in the kitchen when the lights suddenly started flickering. Andreasson's mother, father, and seven children were in the living room when the lights finally went out. It was just past 6:30 PM.

Andreasson was perturbed by bizarre reddish lights that flashed through the kitchen windows. As the sudden darkness enveloped them, and the red lights shone through the front of the house, the children became terrified.

By the sound of her children's distress, Betty fled the kitchen to comfort them, while her father went to investigate the red lights outside. Peering through the kitchen window, Andreasson's father witnessed a spectacular sight: In the glare of the red lights, five strange creatures made their way towards the house.

Mr. Andreasson headed back into the living room in time to see the creatures walk through the family's thick, wooden front door, as if it was nonexistent. His eyes darted to his family — they appeared to be frozen where they stood.

Four of the creatures were around four feet tall with sharp slits for mouths, miniscule ears, wide eyes, small noses, and oblong heads that closely resembled a pear. The fifth creature — which appeared to be the leader of the group — stood at around five feet tall.

Dressed in blue outfits — not unlike a wetsuit, with a board belt and a logo of what looked like a bird on the sleeves — the creatures seemed to be in some sort of uniform, complete with matching pairs of slender boots.

The sleeves of their clothing went all the way down to their three-fingered hands. Although the creatures had legs, they seemed to be floating slightly above the ground.

Mr. Andreasson watched in horror as the leader approached him. It was clear that the four others were having some sort of telepathic conversation with his daughter, Betty. Betty would recall feeling terrified for her children, but at the same time an overwhelming sense of peace and amity fell over her — almost like these beings were old friends of hers.

Betty's fear for her children did not go unnoticed by her guests. At the sign of Betty's mounting hysteria, the creatures released her daughter from her state of suspended animation as a gesture of good will. Comforted by this, Betty followed the beings into her backyard.

Arriving at a deep slope, Betty was greeted by a massive, metallic craft shaped like two inverted saucers, which she estimated to be about 20 feet in diameter. Betty remembers boarding the craft, but not how she did it.

The craft then joined with a larger mother ship, where Betty was subjected to a series of examinations and experimentation that tested how she responded to all kinds of strange equipment. Sometime during these extensive and disturbing procedures, Betty succumbed to a crippling burst of pain that she claims transformed into an ethereal, transcendent experience that bordered on religious.

Four hours later, Betty was escorted back to her home by two of the smaller creatures. Her family was still frozen in place and guarded by one of the creatures that had been left behind. Upon her arrival, the creature released her family.

She later recalled the extraordinary incident in a series of flashes: the power surge, the red lights, the creatures entering through the door. Her memories of what she experienced onboard the alien ship, however, were extremely hazy. Initially, Betty, being a devote and faithful Christian woman, believed that her encounter was acutely religious, and that the creatures were sent as emissaries from God.

With nine witnesses to the strange encounter, Betty's story quickly gained traction among UFO enthusiasts, but it wasn't until 10 years after the encounter, in 1977, that a serious investigation finally took place. Lasting 12 months, Betty went through extensive psychiatric evaluations, lie detector tests, and a total of 14 regressive hypnosis sessions.

A team of experts including a solar physicist, UFO investigator, electrical engineer, aerospace engineer, a hypnotist, and a medical doctor all set forth to test the validity of Betty's story. The results of these tests were documented in a 528 page, three-volume report. The case is still open to this day.

During Betty Andreasson's regressive hypnosis, she speaks in an eerie and awed tone about an entity she referred to as "The One" — though no actual name was mentioned by the beings. Betty relives being transported to a powerful light force which she felt radiated love and compassion.

Lead through a wall of glass so immense that it could not be measured, Betty traveled through a maze of doors, before she was instructed to enter and meet "The One". Betty, in a mind-boggling and dramatic turn of events, remembers seeing herself in front of the door and stepping outside of herself, as if she were split into two people.

At this point in the transcripts, the hypnotist asked Betty to describe "The One", but says she was specifically asked by the being not to do so. When asked what "The One" told her, she claimed she couldn't reveal that, either.

Betty did, however, describe the being that lead her to "The One": a tall, white-haired man in a flowing robe. In an effort to ensure that Betty's memories aligned with the present, the hypnotist asked about her children. Betty replied that she had no children.

It turned out that Betty was relieving an earlier abduction which occurred when she was just 13 years old, and her memories of "The One" were from that very first encounter. When the researchers delved further into Betty's buried memories, the recovered information started painting a disquieting scene.

Beings of over seven feet tall, humanoid, with long white robes, flowing blonde-white hair, and stark white skin — who Betty simply referred to as "The Elders" — appeared to be performing a sort of ritualistic magic. Watching from the sidelines, Betty witnessed three Elders step into a sectioned circle split into six equal parts.

The Elders lifted their hands and joined together. Bizarre beams of light shot from their foreheads and collided in the center of the circle to form a massive, glowing triangle. Inside the triangle was a ring of blinding light.

Another trio entered the circle and created a second triangle that combined with the first to form a perfect hexagon. The bright light intensified and rose, forming an expanding circle around the six Elders' heads. The light rings inside the hexagon then ascended and connected, birthing a sphere of soft-purple light.

The next thing Betty could recall was a small green orb of light that transported her and the white-haired man to a wooded area filled with homeless people. The memories of what happened in the woods, though, were muddled and unclear.

Suddenly, a flash of blistering white light, and they were in a hospital room. An elderly man, who appeared to be inches from death, was surrounded by beings made of a hazy substance, two black and one white light. The beings were after something the man possessed and were apparently struggling to obtain it. The Elder shot an orb of light at the black creatures and they fled.

Afterwards, Betty and the Elder were back in the woods. A silver saucer guarded by two gray creatures was poised and waiting. Betty was then beckoned by one of them. The creature bestowed three balls of light to Betty. In a later interview, Betty remembered the acute sadness she felt at parting with those balls of light.

Both Betty and her daughter remembered many details from the encounter through hypnosis. On top of that, the results of the lie detector and psychiatric tests showed that Betty was sane and, in her mind at least, telling the truth.

Still, being one of the most fantastical and controversial stories of alien contact, Betty's account continues to face skepticism from naysayers and UFO enthusiasts alike.

Chapter 5
The Falcon Lake Landing, 1967

On a beautiful spring afternoon, on May 20, 1967, an industrial mechanic and amateur geologist named Stephen Michalak ventured into the wilderness near Falcon Lake in Manitoba, Canada. There, he experienced what would come to be known as one of the most famous UFO encounters in the history of Canada.

Michalak set out from his home in Winnipeg and traveled to a motel near the Trans-Canada Highway. He was an experienced prospector, and was on his way to the Whiteshell Provincial Park, set on searching the mountainside for riches. After trekking some way into the woods, Michalak stumbled upon a promising quartz vein near a small brook.

While he was examining the vein, at around 12:15 PM, the sound of geese overhead directed his eyes to the sky. No birds could be seen. Instead, Michalak was greeted by a disturbing and unnatural sight.

Two cigar-shaped, red lights glowed brightly in the sky, and seemed to be coming in Michalak's direction. At first, he couldn't quite make them out, but as they swooped closer, the lights proved to be large, disc-shaped vessels of unknown origin.

Flashing from red to orange to gray, the crafts parted ways, one hovering as the other landed about 150 feet from Michalak, on top of a smooth rock. The parked craft was about 35 feet in diameter and appeared to be made of pristine stainless steel with a marked golden glow.

Flashing, colored lights radiated from the inside — so bright that even with Michalak wearing his protective welding glasses, the brilliant lights shocked and irritated his eyes. About 30 minutes after the landing, the acrid smell of sulfur permeated the air. The astonished prospector heard a loud hissing sound, just before a small door slid open on the side of the craft.

Whispered voices seemed to be coming from inside the UFO. Michalak didn't know what to make of the vessel. Assuming that it was some sort of experimental Soviet machine, Michalak proceeded to ask the hushed voices if they spoke Russian.

When he received no response, he used his impressive linguistic skills to ask the same question in English, German, French, Italian, and Ukrainian, only to be met with complete silence — the whispers had now stopped.

Overcome by curiosity, Michalak stepped closer to the craft. Close enough to look inside, he witnessed a maze of bright lights that appeared to be flashing in some sort of sequence on what looked like a control panel. Despite the voices he'd heard, the craft was — at least as far as he could tell — entirely empty.

Michalak — who would later claim that the outside of the craft actually resembled highly-polished glass, devoid of seams or breaks — reached out to touch the exterior of the craft, whereupon he was met with a surface so searing hot that the fingers on his glove instantly melted. Shocked, Michalak quickly removed his glove and was surprised to find that the craft seemed to react to his touch.

The door quickly shut, and the craft shot straight up into the air. What looked to be an exhaust port, around 9 inches high and 6 inches wide, blasted Michalak with scorching-hot air that immediately ignited his clothing. He quickly scrambled to rip his jacket and shirt from his body and stamped out the flames, hoping to avoid a forest fire.

Within a few moments, he suddenly felt deathly ill. In an effort to mark the spot of his encounter, he placed pinecones and branches in an organized manner at the scene. After finally reaching his car, the nausea escalated, and Michalak had to pull over several times on the way back to his hotel room.

The closest hospital was a whole 4 hours from his current location, and the pain was steadily getting worse. With a shaky voice, Michalak phoned his wife and son and asked them to meet him at the bus station in Winnipeg at 10:45 PM. From there, they drove the long way to Misericordia Hospital.

Michalak was admitted for a staggering number of symptoms, including headache, diarrhea, weakness, dizziness, vomiting, hives, numbness, swelling of the joints, eye irritation, and burns. He told the admitting physician that his burns were due to exhaust from an "aeroplane of sorts". In the following weeks, Michalak struggled to eat, and lost an alarming 22 pounds.

In addition to these physiological side effects of his encounter with the unknown craft, his burns were highly abnormal in nature. They had a weird geometrical pattern that resembled grill marks, almost as if he had fallen chest-first onto a fully lit barbeque. Even stranger, after a visit to his local doctor on May 22nd, the burns — oddly enough — faded and then reappeared, as if they were more recent than the date of the encounter at Falcon Lake.

Michalak also had atypical white blood cell levels and an increase in plasma cells. His lymphocyte level dropped from a normal 25% to just around 16%. In the end, 27 different doctors had examined Michalak in an effort to explain his bizarre combination of medical ailments.

Eventually, they all came to a consensus: direct exposure to high levels of radiation. However — to everyone's surprise — on May 23, test results came back which showed no signs of radiation whatsoever.

To make matters worse, Michalak now also suffered from excessive body swelling. Sometimes, the swelling was so immense that his skin bloated straight out of his shirt cuffs. Doctors were just as baffled with this phenomenon and were at a complete loss at what to do. They attributed the swelling to severe allergies of some kind. To what, they didn't know.

Desperate for answers, a team of investigators eager for proof (or to debunk Michalak's story), flew him over Whiteshell Provincial Park in a helicopter, but he had trouble identifying the site from the air. Evidence of radiation was eventually found near a rock outcropping by a swampy area of the forest, in the general vicinity of where Michalak claimed he discovered the craft.

Sure enough, samples from the soil revealed clear signs of radiation. It was of two varieties; a large portion was attributed to a natural uranium ore deposit in the area, but the other radiation source was much harder to pinpoint.

This particular brand of radiation — radium 226 — was a mystery that analysts could not decipher. Its presence was completely unaccounted for — enough of a concern for government officials to temporarily close off that area of the park.

Nearly a year later, new evidence was discovered at the scene of the alleged encounter. Two "W"-shaped silver bars of around 4 and a half inches in length, together with numerous smaller pieces of silver, were found under lichen on the rock where Michalak witnessed the UFO. These bars were made of the highest-quality silver — a purity so high that it was unaccounted for. A layer of quartz appeared to be embedded in the silver and was stuck to the bar with a strange, sticky, unidentified substance.

In August of 1968 — over a year after his run-in with the alien vessel — Michalak was still feeling unwell. Making the journey to a Mayo Clinic in Rochester, Minnesota, he submitted to a series of physical tests.

Later, when he requested his results, he received a suspicious denial letter, stating that he had never been there, even though he possessed cards from the clinic and medical bills in his name. After further petitioning and with signed consent, Michalak was finally able to get ahold of his medical records. The reports filed his illness away as neurodermatitis (an itchy skin disease) and simple syncope (a condition of sudden fainting).

To this day, the Canadian government remains quiet about the investigative reports into Michalak's case, claiming that all of the information is available to the public at the NRC (National Research Council) in Ottawa.

However, the majority of the interesting findings are blatantly missing from the reports, like the documented study of the burned items and the government's ultimate conclusion on the case. In any event, authorities were officially unable to provide evidence to either substantiate or entirely dismiss Michalak's claims.

Stephen Michalak's experience at Falcon Lake is classified as a CE-II, or a close encounter of the second level on two counts. These counts are as follows: physical traces of the encounter at the suspected area, and a witness with clear physiological side effects.

Many aspects of the Falcon Lake Landing cannot be disproved with any certainty. In the mind of many UFO researchers, the evidence speaks for itself.

Chapter 6
The Pascagoula Incident, 1973

On the early night of October 11, 1973, 42-year old Charles Hickson and 19-year old Calvin Parker Jr. were out fishing by the Pascagoula River in Pascagoula, Mississippi. Out of nowhere, Hickson heard what he described as a weird buzzing sound coming from behind.

When he turned around, he was faced with a mysterious egg-shaped object with two big, bluish lights illuminating the front. It was estimated to be between 30 and 40 feet long, 8 to 10 feet tall. The UFO was hovering just above the water, right outside of the riverbank where the two men were standing.

After a few moments, a door opened, and three strange beings began floating towards the two men. The creatures were among some of the most unique ever reported by any contactee. Charles Hickson would later do his best to describe them:

"The head seemed to come directly to the shoulders, and it had something that resembled a nose…on a face. About where ears would be there was something similar to the nose, only, *it was a little longer.*

And under the nose there was something like a slit for a mouth. And it was very wrinkled. It appeared to me to be something like an elephant skin... And in the area where the eyes should have been it was so wrinkled that I'm not even sure there was eyes."

He also reported that they had claw-like hands, and seemed to be just over 5 feet tall. Hickson later speculated that the creatures may have been robots, since he could not recall them having any visible or audible effects of breathing.

Even though Hickson and Parker were both terrified, they were not able to run away. Inexplicably, they both found themselves completely paralyzed. After hovering to where the stunned fishermen were standing, two of the beings grabbed Hickson while the third took care of Parker — who had fainted out of pure shock.

They made their way to a bright lit room inside the hovering UFO, where Hickson was left floating, as if laying on an invisible bed. Still paralyzed, he could not move any part of his body except his eyes. A strange device which looked like a big, almond shaped, robotic eye went over his body as if it was scanning him. After the device retracted, Hickson was left alone for some time, presumably because the beings were then tending to Parker.

Eventually, Hickson was floated back onto the pier where Parker now stood, seemingly in shock. Then, the object rose straight into the sky and flew away quietly. Hickson later estimated that the whole extraordinary ordeal took no more than 20 minutes.

Hickson — while startled by the event — was a veteran of the Korean war, and handled it much better than the younger Calvin Parker Jr.

49

Charles Hickson stated in an interview:

"The only thing I remember is that kid, Calvin, just standing there. I've never seen that sort of fear on a man's face as I saw on Calvin's. It took me a while to get him back to his senses, and the first thing I told him was, son, ain't nobody gonna believe this. Let's just keep this whole thing to ourselves."

After the incident, the two men sat in Hickson's car, trying to calm themselves and make sense of what just happened. They were afraid of public ridicule and were unsure of whether or not they should tell someone.

After some time spent regaining their focus, they began thinking about what could happen if the creatures had malevolent intentions. What if other people in the area were being abducted as well? What if this was happening elsewhere, and it was a threat to national security?

They finally decided to contact the Keesler Air Force Base in Biloxi, Mississippi. The sergeant who answered their phone call told them that the Air Force no longer (officially, anyway) investigated UFOs. They were instructed to contact their local sheriff department instead.

Hickson and Parker drove the long way to the Jackson County, Mississippi Sheriff's office, where they met Sheriff Fred Diamond and Captain Glenn Ryder, who conducted interviews with the two men.

Sheriff Diamond was understandably skeptical of their story, and was carefully looking for any signs of hoaxing. Still, the men — in particular Parker — seemed genuinely frightened and disturbed, which made the Sheriff curious. He decided he would treat the case seriously and get to the bottom of it all.

After being interviewed separately, Parker and Hickson were placed together in a room which — unbeknownst to them — was wired for sound. There, they talked privately. Their conversations were recorded and a tape was produced, which the Sheriff suspected would prove their story to be a hoax. To his amazement, however, he discovered that the two men acted even more disturbed than when they were talking to the authorities one by one.

After their interviews at the sheriff's office, Hickson and Parker decided to keep completely quiet about the event. They went to work at the local shipyard the following morning. Stressed and sleep deprived, they went through their workday, without a mention of what they had experienced the previous night. A few hours after punching in, Sheriff Fred Diamond called the men at work, informing them that reporters were questioning him, trying to uncover more information about the extraordinary event.

Despite their best efforts to keep the story under wraps, the mainstream media was quickly alerted to their case. Much to the dismay of the two men, their story had spread across the globe in a matter of days. Their home town of *Gautier, Mississippi suddenly* became inundated by astronomers, reporters, UFO enthusiasts and independent researchers.

While already under much stress due to the overwhelming media attention, the two men also became concerned about a possible radiation exposure during their encounter inside the flying object. They initially requested to be checked at the local hospital, but they lacked the necessary equipment.

Instead, they ended up at Keesler Air Force Base, the very same facility which had turned them down when they first reported their experience with the ETs. There, they were thoroughly examined by several medical professionals who found no signs of radiation poisoning.

Following the radiation test, the military intelligence chief of the base requested to meet with them. Both Parker and Hickson were interviewed by him while many others observed the proceedings. Later in the evening, an Air Force artist also made a sketch of one of the creatures, based on Hickson's recollections.

The Pascagoula incident eventually gained the attention of the Aerial Phenomena Research Organization (APRO), a UFO research group which consisted of many scientists, and put much emphasis on scientific field investigations. They sent James A. Harder, a University of California engineering professor, to investigate the case. He teamed up with the famed Dr. J. Allen Hynek, who represented the U.S. Air Force, and together they interviewed Hickson and Parker extensively.

Harder attempted to perform regressive hypnosis on Charles Hickson, but the session was interrupted as he became too terrified to continue. Additionally, both Hickson and Parker took polygraph tests, which they passed. After ending their investigation, both Harder and Hynek concluded that both of the contactees were telling the truth.

J. Allen Hynek later stated in an interview:

"I went down to Pascagoula completely negative, but I worked with those men for quite a while. I listened to tapes that had been taken when they didn't know they were being

*taped. I saw how Charlie behaved under hypnosis, and finally, the lie detector test. All of those things convinced me that he was not making it up. They had had **an** experience, period."*

According to an old article in the MUFON (Mutual UFO Network) journal, a sonic boom was heard across the mid-western and eastern part of the United States an hour or so before the contact at Pascagoula. Additionally, a large number of UFO sightings took place in the following days and weeks after this mysterious boom.

In the decades that followed, new information emerged which seemed to validate Parker and Hickson's story. In 2001, retired navy chief petty officer Mike Cataldo, revealed that he and his crew mates Ted Peralta and Mack Hanna observed a UFO around the Pascagoula area the same night as the Hickson & Parker contact.

He described it as *"a large tambourine with small flashing lights"*. The UFO reportedly crossed the freeway before it hovered over a tree line and disappeared from sight.

"Puddin" Broadus, a local Pascagoula detective, also reported seeing something unusual fly through the air that night. He allegedly witnessed a flash of greenish light, which was also seen by a man named Larry Booth, who was operating a service station nearby.

The Pascagoula incident is briefly mentioned in the channeled work "The Law of One", also known as "The Ra Material". According to this material (allegedly relayed by highly-evolved ETs), the beings who contacted Hickson and Parker were from the Sirius star system. They were peaceful, vegetation-like lifeforms which evolved from something similar to a tree (which would explain their unusual appearance and lack of noticeable breathing).

It further states that the beings were recording the life experience of Charlie Hickson in order to learn, taking a special interest in his time during the Korean war. These entities were said to be mostly existing in a near-meditative state, and a life of constant movement (and aggressive behavior) such as ours were foreign to them.

Consequently, to these beings, Hickson's mind became a valuable subject of contemplation. It also mentions that he agreed, during his pre-incarnate, or between-lives state, to be available for such a service.

The aftermath of the Pascagoula incident would influence the men in different ways. In the years following the incident,

Calvin Parker Jr. mostly avoided the public eye. He was rather negatively affected by what happened, and frequently struggled with sleep deprivation and sudden-onset anxiety. At one point he was even hospitalized due to an emotional breakdown.

Hickson, while cautious at first, eventually learned to accept his role in the spotlight. He initially appeared on television shows like "The Tonight Show" with Johnny Carson and "The Dick Cavett Show". Later, he went on to co-author a book with William Mendez about his experience, titled "UFO Contact at Pascagoula".

He also directed a documentary called "In Contact", and did numerous conferences and radio interviews. As he looked back on the encounter later in his life, Hickson felt that the beings who took him aboard that vessel that fateful night were actually benevolent, and felt that spreading the message of interplanetary intelligence and possible future cooperation between races was important.

As a result of his encounter, Hickson also started advocating for environmental sustainability and ending all conflict between human beings.

On September 9, 2011, Charles Hickson passed away at the age of 80. His story is, to this day, one of the most intriguing alien contact cases of modern times. Despite living through ridicule and frequent stress due to the large attention, Hickson always stood by his word. His fascinating story remained the same until the day he died.

Chapter 7
The Medicine Bow Encounter, 1974

On October 25, 1974, Carl Higdon — an oil driller, husband, and father of four — packed the company pickup truck and headed out to Medicine Bow National Forest in search of food for his family. It was during the recession, and many families were struggling to put food on the table.

Higdon invested in a brand-new Magnum rifle, complete with powerful 7-millimeter bullets, and planned to scout out some elk to keep his loved ones fed through the winter. Higdon ran into an old friend on the way into the woods, who told him of an area where he'd seen several large elk. Higdon followed his friend's advice and made his way to the northern section of the park.

He didn't have to wait long before five massive elk strolled into his range. The hunter took aim with his scope and shot. He waited for the painful recoil, the sound of the bullet detonation, but was instead met with an inexplicable silence.

There was no kickback, no snick of the bullet leaving the gun, but Higdon was able to watch the bullet's trajectory. The bullet moved at a snail's pace, as if it was being manipulated by some unknown force. The bullet made it about 50 feet before it froze and dropped to the snowy ground, not even remotely close to hitting the herd of elk.

Higdon stood there, puzzled and disturbed by his gun's apparent malfunction, unable to do more than stare at the bullet nestled in the snow. After a few moments, he recovered the bullet and placed it in a canvas pocket. As soon as he touched it, a weird tingling sensation traveled up his body.

A snap of a tree branch jolted him back to reality. Higdon lifted his gaze in the direction of the sound and was faced with a humanoid creature unlike anything he'd ever seen before.

Standing over 6 feet tall, dressed in what looked like a black jumpsuit with a wide belt and what appeared to be a harness that crisscrossed over its chest, the creature looked as if he was wearing some kind of uniform. The belt was emblazoned with a six-pointed star and a yellow emblem that Higdon couldn't identify.

The strange humanoid terrified the hunter. Its skin was yellow cast, its face disappeared straight into its neck without any definition — no chin, no jaw. Straw-like hair stood straight up on the top of its head, and its eyebrows were nonexistent.

The being stood bowlegged but tall and, instead of hands where its arms ended, there were pointed appendages that closely resembled a tool like a rod or drill. In a later instance of hypnotic memory regression, Higdon recalled that the humanoid creature looked to have had no more than six teeth — three up top and three on the bottom. Higdon also recalled that the creature was a male, and was named "Ausso One".

Ausso One apparently spoke English, though its communications may have been telepathic in nature, as Higdon couldn't remember any mouth movement during their conversations.

The alien being asked Higdon if he was hungry, since he was sneaking up on elk in the forest. Evidence from hypnosis showed a lengthier conversation between the two, where the ET asked if Higdon would like to go with him, to which the hunter replied by shrugging his shoulders.

Higdon admitted that he was hungry and Ausso told him of some pills he had, and that if he ate one, he wouldn't have to eat for about four days. Ausso proceeded to throw Higdon a container filled with four of these strange pills. In an unprecedented move, Higdon swallowed the pill almost immediately. In his day-to-day life, he was known to abhor pills, and even refused medications as common as aspirin.

Ausso gestured toward Higdon and, at this point, Higdon noticed a transparent box-like craft that floated above the ground. In the blink of an eye, Higdon was transported into what he assumed was the craft he'd seen near Ausso. Higdon found himself encased in a small area and strapped down to a chair.

Bands were cinched tight around his arm, and a helmet with cords that plugged into the top —which lead somewhere he couldn't see — was strapped to his head. Perpendicular to his newfound prison, a console with levers of various sizes was visible.

From a mirror lodged close to his head, Higdon was able to see the five elk he'd been hunting herded together in some sort of cage — they did not seem to move a muscle. Two other humanoid creatures like Ausso were also inside the craft. As they rose higher into the air, Higdon spotted what he thought was planet Earth, far beneath him.

Ausso informed him that they were flying to his home planet, which was located 163,000 light years from Earth. Seconds later, they had arrived. With a lift of his hand, Ausso transported Higdon from the craft onto a central square. A tall, metallic cityscape that looked like a futuristic Seattle skyline flooded his view. Each skyscraper-style building radiated with the light from a sun that was far more powerful than he'd ever felt on Earth.

The staggering brightness automatically made his eyes burn and water; he reached up to shade his eyes from the light. A gigantic tower of 90 feet in height with a rotating, domed, light system stood directly in front of Higdon. The whirring of the building sounded like an electric razor.

Higdon was perplexed to find five normal-looking humans casually chatting by the alien tower. Higdon described them as a gray-haired 40-50-year old male, a brunette girl of around 10 or 11, a blonde girl between 13 and 14, and a couple that appeared to be between 17 and 18. They were all wearing regular, Earth-like clothing.

Ausso One pointed again, and suddenly Higdon was inside a box-like chamber which he felt may have been an elevator. In an instant, Higdon was in a new room, propped up on a shelf-like device with something that resembled a shield which popped out of the wall.

After about four minutes, the shield-like object receded and Ausso told Higdon that "he was not what they needed". Ausso then pulled a kind of lever and, just like that, Higdon was teleported away from the peculiar environment.

He landed hard on a 9-foot high decline in Medicine Bow Park. Unable to get his bearings, Higdon tripped over a rock and plummeted down the slope, whacking his head, neck, and shoulders. Two and a half hours had elapsed since he met the strange being called Ausso One.

Disoriented, scared, and perplexed by what transpired, Higdon searched frantically for his truck, but it was not where he left it. Higdon found the pickup three miles from where he'd parked it, in an inexplicable condition. The pickup was now situated in a mud-filled sinkhole.

Unable to free the truck, Higdon used his CB radio to call the local Sheriff's office. The police got to the scene at around midnight and were stunned by what they found. There were no tracks leading up to the hole. Rather, it looked as though the vehicle had been picked up and dropped from above. Meanwhile, Higdon was inconsolable and frantic, shouting, "they took my elk!" repeatedly.

He was eventually admitted into Carbon County Memorial Hospital in Rawlings, New York at 2:30 AM on October 26, 1974. Higdon had trouble recognizing his wife, but was not listed as having a concussion.

In fact, other than bloodshot eyes that watered nonstop, he seemed to be in better health than he'd ever been. Tests showed that his vitamin levels were elevated, the kidney stones he'd had prior to the incident had miraculously vanished, and all scarring on his lungs from a bout of tuberculosis was completely gone.

Other notable evidence was eyewitness accounts by Higdon's wife and two other people, who saw red-green flashing lights in the general vicinity of where Higdon encountered Ausso One. The most compelling finding, however, was the bullet that never met its target.

The bullet was deformed in a way that was impossible to decipher. The lug was missing entirely and the jacket was inversed — like it had been flipped inside out in a single motion. A specialist who had examined the bullet had never seen anything like it, and stated that it would have taken tremendous force to morph the bullet into that position.

On November 2, 1974, Higdon was subjected to four hours of interviews, as well as several attempts at hypnosis which were unsuccessful. Two weeks later, on November 17th, the memory regression finally succeeded. Higdon was able to remember extensive conversations with Ausso One, predominantly about the reason for visiting Earth.

Ausso confessed that the sun's rays on his planet had become so strong that several species of animals had died out. This was also the reason for the black body suits, he said, which protected the ETs from the scorching rays of their star.

Ausso's people were reportedly on Earth to look for alternative food sources, as well as securing individuals from various species of animals for "breeding purposes" back on their planet. Higdon speculated that the humans he saw on the alien planet may also have been part of some sort of breeding initiative, as all of them looked to be young and fertile.

This would also explain why he was told that he "was not what they needed", after he appeared to be scanned by the strange shield-like contraption. Higdon had in fact undergone a vasectomy a few years prior to his unexpected trip to the alien world.

For weeks after the incident, Higdon was convinced that a bright, green light was stalking him. Hyper paranoid and hysterical, Higdon maintained that the ETs were regularly checking up on him.

In September of 1978, Higdon took a PSE: psychological stress evaluation through the LAPD under a psychiatrist named Dr. Greenburg. The results of the polygraph were crystal clear, Higdon was — at least in his own mind — telling the truth about what he experienced that fateful day in Medicine Bow.

Chapter 8
The Allagash Abductions, 1976

The Allagash Wilderness Waterway is an area in Maine, a state in the New England region of the United States of America. It is a large, beautiful territory of lakes, ponds, rivers and streams going through the middle of northern Maine's thick forests.

It was in this area that four men's quiet fishing trip turned into a mind-boggling, paranormal event. An event which would haunt their dreams and distorted memories in the years which followed.

In late August of 1976, twin brothers Jim and Jack Weiner, together with their friends Charlie Foltz and Chuck Rak, went on vacation to Allagash. All of the four men were former art students who had met each other at the Massachusetts College of Art.

They started their vacation on August 20, and spent the next several days hiking and canoeing along the waterway, enjoying each other's company and the peaceful landscape which surrounded them. On the evening of August 26, they reached an area known as Eagle Lake, and proceeded to set up camp.

They got out their fishing rods and tried their luck by the bank, but nothing bit. They agreed to relocate to the middle of the lake for some night fishing, as it was quickly getting dark. Before heading out onto the water they made a large bonfire, in order to highlight their campsite so they easily could find their way back.

A short while after they had settled the canoe and started fishing, Chuck Rak felt as though he was being intently watched. He turned around, and observed a massive, multi-colored sphere of light emerging above the southeastern tree line — approximately 200 yards away from the canoe. The object was completely soundless while moving. Parts of it would change color in a *"plasmatic motion"* as it moved. First red to green, then from green to a light yellow. According to the men's estimations, it was about 80 feet in diameter.

After being stunned for a second, Chuck yelled for the others to turn around. Startled but intrigued, Charlie Foltz took out his flashlight and used it to signal an "SOS" in the direction of the mysterious object. The sphere instantly changed direction, and started moving slowly towards the four men.

As it approached, the UFO started emitting a hollow beam of light. As the beam hit the water surface near them, the men panicked and began paddling frantically to get away. While adrenalin pumped through their veins, they focused all their attention on their bonfire in the distance, but it was too late. The beam of light fully enveloped the four friends and their canoe.

The next thing they knew, they were all standing by the campsite at the shore, looking at the illuminated object now rising into the sky, about 50 to 70 yards away from them. The sphere then shot into the far distance in the blink of an eye — still completely silent.
The men simply stood there for a while, watching the night

sky, unable to speak. The intense panic which they had felt in their previously-remembered moments was now gone. Confused, they wondered: Had they "blacked out" due to the effects of the adrenalin rush, and carried themselves to the shore?

Their minds were also inexplicably in a numb, dreamy state — as if they had just woken up from a deep level of anesthesia. As they were starting to regain their normal senses, they noticed that the large bonfire — which was burning brightly just minutes ago — was now nothing more than hot ashes and red coal.

They had placed large logs in the fire so that it would burn for several hours yet — to their knowledge — they had been away for no more than 20 minutes. This would remain a mystery for the four men, as they ended their vacation and returned home to their newly-formed careers.

Eventually, however, the UFO encounter would be shown to affect them on a subconscious level. What at first seemed to "merely" have been a close-up sighting would increasingly be revealed as something much more bizarre.

Several years after the extraordinary event, Jim Weiner received a head injury which resulted in temporal lobe epilepsy — a neurological condition which often includes sensory changes and disturbances of memory. During a checkup, his doctors asked him if he had any noteworthy experiences which may have been related to his condition.

Jim proceeded to reluctantly tell the doctors about him and his friends' close encounter with the mysterious glowing sphere and the feeling of missing time, as well as the continued, intense nightmares which had haunted everyone in the group ever since. His brother, Jack Weiner, was the first to have these vivid dreams.

During these nightmares, they saw strange beings with large heads and long necks. The descriptions of the entities' faces are reminiscent of the classic "Grey alien" variant. They had very large, lidless eyes which had a slight glow to them, and which seemed to be covered by a thin, metallic surface.

Their hands were said to be insect-like, with only four fingers on each one. They had very small nostrils, and simple slits for mouths. Jack Weiner saw flashes of the beings examining his arm while his friends were seated nearby — seemingly paralyzed.

The doctors suspected that Jim and his group might have been involved in an alien abduction, and advised him to contact a

UFO researcher. In 1988, Jim went to a UFO conference hosted by the author and researcher Raymond Fowler. After the conference, Jim met with Fowler and told him everything about the paranormal incident. Fowler was highly intrigued, noting that a multiple-witness case like this was incredibly rare. He decided to help Jim and his friends find some answers.

In January of 1989, he started a formal investigation together with MUFON investigator and solar physicist, David Webb, and MUFON consultant and professional hypnotist, Anthony Constantino. Together, they carefully studied the men and their extraordinary accounts during a period of two years.

It started with several, detailed psychiatric tests and examinations, which resulted in all of the men being deemed mentally stable. In addition, all of them took lie detector tests, which they all passed.

Finally, they underwent a series of regressive hypnosis sessions conducted by Constantino. During these sessions, which Constantino described as *"The most intense experience I've had as a hypnotist"*, a great deal of new information came to light.

During the hypnosis, all of the witnesses revealed that they had been transferred into the illuminated sphere by the hollow beam of light which enveloped them. Once onboard, the strange creatures from their dreams had them under some sort of mind control, which rendered them in a kind of tranquilized state. All of them were made to undress, before they were examined one by one on a silvery table.

The beings then used several hand-held and machine-like instruments to analyze the men. During the examination, they apparently took samples of different bodily fluids such as blood, urine and sperm, as well as skin scrapings. After the tests concluded, the men were made to put on their clothes again, before lining up near a round portal in another section of the UFO.

They were then levitated back onto the canoe below, and accurately placed in each of the positions they were sitting in prior to the abduction. When the hypnosis sessions were concluded, it was discovered that all of the four men's recollections of the event were consistent with each other.

In 1993, Raymond Fowler stated in an article:
"During the course of the investigation we conducted witness background checks, examined medical records and diaries, cross-checked witness testimony, coordinated witness psychological profile tests, correlated witness accounts with

other reports and conducted fifteen hypnosis sessions over a period of 14 months. The final 10-volume report numbered over 700 pages.

...The investigation concluded that the moral character of the witnesses, the graphic reliving of their experiences under hypnosis and the extraordinary correlations between their experience and that of others, provided overwhelming evidence that their experiences were objective in nature.

Such evidence, combined with typical physical effects on the witnesses' bodies, prompted me to evaluate this case in the "great significance" category."

Chapter 9
The Dechmont Woods Encounter, 1979

On a cool November morning, Robert Taylor, a 61-year-old forester from West Lothian, Scotland, hopped in his work truck with his dog — an energetic, red setter — and made his way to Dechmont Law. An employee of the Livingston Development Corporation, Taylor was very familiar with the area. He left his house at around 10:30 AM on November 5, 1979 in order to double check the progress of some saplings for the company.

The saplings were situated a short way into a secluded forest off the M8 Motorway. When Robert Taylor got in his truck that morning for routine-work maintenance with his dog, never in a million years could he have guessed that his life would be forever altered. The story of what happened that morning has perplexed countless UFO researchers for decades.

Taylor parked his pickup truck at the head of the forest trail and set off on foot, together with his canine friend. After walking for a while, he made it to a clearing where he was stopped dead in his tracks. There, hovering in mid-air, was a large, spherical object about 20 feet across and 12 feet tall.

The craft appeared abrasive and dark, like black sandpaper. It floated in absolute silence, suspended, as if frozen in position. Taylor gaped at the object, taking in the small, round windows that seemed to circle above a protruding ring that looked like the rim of a hat.

As he watched, the object flickered in color, pieces fading to near transparency and then filling back in, as if the craft was attempting to enter some sort of invisibility mode.

Awe-struck by the astonishing sight in front of him, Taylor recoiled from the craft as two smaller sphere-like objects with metal spikes that reminded him of old Navy mines burst from the larger vessel. The spiked spheres began to roll towards him, leaving distinct impressions in the soil.

Taylor was frozen in absolute shock at the bizarre scene — so startled that he didn't have time to react as the two spheres latched on to his pant legs. The spherical objects pulled Taylor towards the larger craft with a force so powerful that his heels scraped and tore into the ground. The spheres then released toxic, acrid smelling fumes that made him gag, and which invaded his senses to the point that he lost consciousness.

The next thing he knew, Taylor woke up face down on the grass to the sound of his dog barking in a panicked state — racing frantically around the clearing. Taylor tried to speak in an effort to calm his distraught dog, but found that his voice was completely gone.

Hoping to offer his dog some comfort, Taylor attempted to stand, but found that he had lost all semblance of physical strength. He desperately crawled toward his truck as he gradually regained his energy, before he eventually managed to pick himself up and get in the driver's seat.

When Taylor reached his truck he was still disoriented, and ended up driving it into a bank of wet mud. Unable to dislodge the pickup, Taylor — covered in mud and looking worse for wear — made the long journey home on foot. When Taylor finally made it to the door of his house, his wife was disturbed by his appearance, as she thought he had been assaulted.

Still reeling from his life-altering encounter, Taylor was uncertain about calling the police and instead dialed his job supervisor, Malcolm Drummond. Taylor then recounted his full story from the comfort of his bathtub.

Malcolm Drummond was convinced by his colleague's passionate tale and the two deep scrapes that he showed him as evidence. He decided to follow him to the location in the Dechmont Woods to investigate the scene of this extraordinary event. Urged on by his wife, Taylor finally phoned the police, who ended up accompanying them.

At the site, the soil was rife with strange markings that could not be explained by any typical machinery. The markings were checked against all the forestry vehicles that would have been exposed to the area, which resulted in no matches being found. The tears found on Taylor's pants were also impossible to identify. The fabric had clearly been pierced by an object that effectively pulled upward, as if lifting Taylor off the ground.

Further investigations revealed more mysteries which sparked even more questions that failed to be answered. Police sifted through reports from both the military and civilian flight logs and were shocked to find that not a single aircraft had flown over the area on the morning of November 5, 1979.

Furthermore, no person in the area had reported spotting the strange craft leaving the area. All in all, there were no signs that the vessel had ever left the location, at least, not visually.

A thorough inspection of the clearing where Taylor encountered the spherical craft yielded additional evidence. There were three distinct imprints that validated Taylor's story. The first of these markings were two parallel tracks that looked like a ladder. Each track was 8 feet long and 8 feet apart from the other track.

The second was a bizarre scattering of some 40 small holes that circled the tracks. These holes appeared to be about 4 inches across. Whether or not these holes matched the tearing on Taylor's clothing, or if they could have been from the smaller spherical objects, has either never been investigated or the findings have mysteriously disappeared from public sources.

The final piece of evidence at the scene was a massive indentation in the soil that suggested that something weighing several tons had rested on the ground there. An alternative explanation as to what could have made this enormous imprint has yet to be found.

UFO investigators have mapped out a timeline of the events in Dechmont forest, estimating that Robert Taylor was knocked unconscious for nearly 20 minutes. What occurred in that time span, however, remains a mystery to this day. When Taylor woke, the large craft and its smaller counterparts had all vanished.

No medical evidence is available to corroborate Taylor's extraordinary story. While he did attempt to go to the hospital with his wife, the wait was so long, and they were given the runaround so many times, that they ended up leaving without seeing a doctor.

To this day, the Dechmont Woods case remains open and unsolved.

Chapter 10
The Rendlesham Forest Incident, 1980

Known as "Britain's Roswell", the Rendlesham Forest Incident has been in the media from time to time ever since the early 1980's. Rendlesham Forest is located just east of Ipswich in Suffolk, England.

To the west of the 5.8-mile wide pine forest was the Royal Air Force (RAF) base Woodbridge, while the RAF Bentwaters was situated along the northern and eastern area of Rendlesham. The United States Air Force was stationed at the two bases at the time, under Wing Commander Colonel Gordon E. Williams. US Air Force lieutenant colonel Charles I. Halt was the deputy commander of the US Airbase in Suffolk, and the base commander was Colonel Ted Conrad.

The extraordinary series of events first started on December 26, 1980 when Staff Sergeant Bud Steffens and Airman First Class John Burroughs, security personnel of the US Air Force, were stationed at the east gate of the RAF base in Woodbridge. Just past midnight, James 'Jim' Penniston was informed by Steffens of odd illuminations in the sky just above the

Rendlesham Forest.

Penniston got confirmation from radar operators in Bentwaters about the presence of an object that flew 60 miles in just two or three seconds — equivalent to thousands of miles per hour. The lightning-fast UFO then came back, stopped near a water tower and proceeded to hover over the forest. Penniston remembered thinking that whatever the object was, it was clearly under intelligent control.

The lights then slowly descended into the forest. Thinking that an aircraft crash landed, three military personnel were deployed to investigate the scene. Sgt. Steffens later confirmed that the craft *"didn't crash... it landed."* The three who responded were Penniston, John Burroughs, and an airman named Edward N. Cabansag.

While traversing the east gate road on their way to the site of the presumed crash, they could see the different-colored lights moving in the woods before settling in a position amongst the trees.

The three men slumped onto the ground for cover as it dawned on them that there was no plane to be found. It was still dark at the time, but the forest was somehow lit up. The animals at a nearby farm went crazy and were making a lot of noise —

obviously sensing something was amiss.

The men got up and continued their approach. They climbed the fence separating the forest and the open field, and walked toward the source of the white light — which was now located somewhere near the farmer's house.

As they got nearer, their radios started acting up. Cabansag was told to find an area without disturbance, so he could use it to relay transmissions back to the control center. While Cabansag split from the group, Penniston and Burroughs continued walking towards the strange craft.

The men didn't find any debris from a wreckage. There was no fire or any other sign that something had crash landed in the forest. What they did find was, as described by Penniston after the incident, *"a craft of unknown origin"*. Up close, he saw blue and yellow lights and hieroglyphic-like characters on the metallic exterior of the 9 feet tall and 9 feet wide object. A red, pulsing light could also be seen on its top.

Penniston further relayed that the craft had no landing gear. He was able to come close enough to touch the craft — which he described as black, smooth, opaque, and warm. He claimed he had a camera with him and that he used all 36 shots. Penniston later detailed in the 2014 book, "Encounter in

Rendlesham Forest" that what he saw *"was not an aircraft which could have been manufactured in 1980, or even now"*.

45 minutes into their investigation, the lights on the craft became brighter. The men were taken aback. The craft then silently floated off the ground, deftly made its way through the trees, and darted away at an "impossible" speed. Just like that, the UFO was gone.

The men went back to base to report their experience and to submit evidence. Among the it was Penniston's logbook where he wrote down details about the encounter and the craft. Unfortunately, the photos from two rolls of films were overexposed.

Around 4 in the morning of the day of the encounter, the local police arrived. They didn't see any strange lights. All they saw were the lights coming from the Orford Ness lighthouse.

The investigation of the scene — conducted on the morning of December 26 by a group that included Captain Mike Verrano and Master Sergeant Ray Gulyas — revealed scorch marks and broken branches on the trees, while a perfect triangle-shaped impression was found where the craft reportedly landed. Additionally, the radiation level on the site was *"significantly higher than the average background"*, according to the scientists from the Ministry of Defence (MoD).

The police were again asked to investigate, but dismissed the indentations as something animals might have done. A photo of the triangular indentation has become one of the most striking pieces of evidence which suggests that alien craft have actually landed on Earth's surface.

This apparent landing, however, would prove to only be the first in a series of extraordinary events which would take place in the area in a span of three days. Two nights after the authorities had finished up examining the initial landing, another group of military personnel witnessed an even more astonishing event.

Sergeant Adrian Bustinza and Larry Warren were among a group of military men sent to investigate the new sighting. When they reached the site, Warren saw an object on the ground which was surrounded by disaster-preparedness officers equipped with Geiger counters — carefully measuring the area for radiation.

Warren recalled that a small, red light appeared from the object and stopped around 20 feet from the ground. Then, the glow of the red orb quickly intensified and suddenly exploded outwards in a harmless burst of light. Another witness,

Sergeant Monroe Nevels — a Disaster Preparedness Technician who worked at the scene that night — saw a total of three lights, with the largest one acting like the leader or command vessel. According to him, the lights seemed to be crafts that flew independently of each other.

When the men finally gathered their wits after witnessing the amazing spectacle involving the lights, they saw a strange object which had landed nearby. As far as the men could tell, there were no windows or markings on it. Warren and Bustinza gave way as Wing Commander Williams advanced towards the unknown object.

Warren looked on as Williams had a silent stand-off with a being from within the craft. He described the strange creature as wearing bright clothing adorned with various small devices, standing around 4 feet tall with a child-like body. He could also make out its very large, black eyes staring at the Wing Commander.

The deputy commander Charles I. Halt was also present when the second encounter occurred. He was ready this time, though; he brought along a dictation device to record what they were doing and saying. He taped a total of 18 minutes of audio recordings.

Halt was heard on the recording saying:
"Okay, we're looking at the thing; were probably about two to three hundred yards away. It looks like an eye winking at you… and the flash is so bright to the star scope that it almost burns your eye."

Before the men could fully take in the amazing experience with the alien being, the craft started hovering a bit and then went straight up in the air before making a sharp 45 degree turn. All that was left was a cold draft and a lot of bewildered minds. Bustinza, in an interview with the late UFO researcher Georgina Bruni, said that the strange craft was "*going in and out through the trees, and at one stage it was hovering.*"

Some skeptics argue that the objects seen over Rendlesham could have been any of the following: a downed aircraft, a helicopter carrying a replica of the Apollo capsule, light coming from the Orford Ness lighthouse (as claimed by the official statement released by the British government), a secret military test, or even a prank by the airmen at the nearby base.

Some astronomers claim that the lights were in fact natural debris from space burning up and becoming a fireball as it entered the Earth's atmosphere somewhere over southern England. These theories, however, leave a lot to be desired. They fail to account for the moving orbs of light, the perfectly triangular indentation on the ground and — the most striking event of all — the face to face contact with an apparent extraterrestrial.

The events that transpired in 1980 continue to baffle and amaze people even today. Interestingly, reports of sightings in the area did not end after those incredible nights in the 80s. In fact, as recent as in early 2015, a man who was out walking his dog saw a series of inexplicable orbs of light hovering over the Rendlesham Forest. If there was ever any investigation into these new sightings, however, is unknown.

A man by the name of Nick Pope worked for the Ministry of Defence from 1985 to 2006. During his time with the government, Pope claimed to have had firsthand information regarding numerous UFO investigations. He was tasked with investigating the sightings and figuring out if they posed a threat to the country. The British government eventually shut down his department, however — forcing him to resign.

Still, that did not deter Pope from becoming a freelance journalist, dealing mostly with UFOs and other mysterious events which went silently by most of the mainstream media. Though he wasn't with the MoD when the encounters happened, he insists that an actual UFO landed in the forest and hat they were not just some vague lights in the sky.

Charles I. Halt recently came up with new evidence of the UFO landing. According to written statements he gathered from the radar operators based at the time at the Bentwaters headquarters and at the neighboring Wattisham Airfield, there were indeed strange objects flying within the vicinity, which they reportedly tracked for some time.

Halt further expressed that this new evidence only came to light now because many of the witnesses waited until they retired before talking about their experiences, for fear of getting punished by their superiors. To this day, Penniston (who along with Burroughs suffered from Post-Traumatic Stress Disorder in the years following the event) and a host of other witnesses, insist that a UFO did indeed land within the Rendlesham Forest.

Chapter 11
UFO Attack On the Knowles Family, 1988

There are certain places in the United States where UFO sightings occur more frequently than elsewhere. The rather arid locations in particular — like in certain areas of California and Arizona — seem to be hotbeds of UFO activity. With this in mind, do the ETs prefer to operate away from most of humanity?

Or perhaps the more vacant terrain simply makes it easier to spot them, resulting in more reports of sightings? Whatever the case may be, vast, dry landscapes often go hand in hand with plentiful observations of mysterious flying objects. This is also the case in some other parts of the world, such as the great Outback "Down Under".

In 1988, an Australian family, the Knowles, were driving on their way to meet with family in Melbourne. Sean Knowles, who was driving the car, was together with his two brothers Patrick and Wayne, their mother Faye, and their two family dogs.

They were riding along the road of Nullarbor Plain, a large desert area in the southern part of Australia when, suddenly, very strange things started happening.

Around 1:30 AM, the music from the family's car speakers became distorted, before the radio finally malfunctioned completely. Around 15 minutes later, the family could see a large light approaching from a distance. At first, they simply assumed it was a big truck with a busted headlight.

As it came closer and closer, it became apparent that there was indeed a truck moving towards them. To their surprise, however, the single, bright light they observed from a distance was actually situated *above* the vehicle. At this point it was clear that the truck was driving in a wild manner, at an immense speed and at the wrong side of the road!

A violent collision was clearly imminent. Sean Knowles, out of pure reflex, managed to quickly turn the car out of the way, and the truck, followed by the hovering ball of light, barely missed their trajectory. He slowed down the car as the stunned family tried to make sense of the incident. Before they could calm their nerves, a station wagon went past them, also accompanied by the bright ball of light overhead. At this point they were puzzled, and wanted answers.

Sean turned the car around and started chasing the mysterious luminescence. While they were beginning to gain on the car and the light, the mother, Faye, had a gut feeling that something was amiss. She pleaded for Sean to disengage, and so he did. He promptly did a U-turn, and they were on their way to Melbourne once again. They all agreed that they would report the incident to the authorities at the next available phone station. However, as you might suspect, the story didn't end there.

Just moments after turning the car around, Sean watched in the rear view mirror as the ball of light now headed towards *them* at a blazing speed. Everyone in the car were gripped by fear, and screamed and pleaded to Sean to get out of there. He increased the speed, but to no avail.

Suddenly, a loud thump could be heard from above. Something heavy apparently landed on top of the roof, as the vehicle bounced slightly downwards from the resulting pressure. Then, the car started slowly elevating into the air. The family panicked in fear for their lives and the dogs both went nuts, but there was nowhere for them to run — they were all trapped.

The object was now levitating the car completely off the ground, propelling them forward at around 120 miles per hour. Faye, who was sitting in the backseat, decided to roll up her window and then desperately tried to dislodge the object. To her great surprise, instead of a metallic feel, her hand was met with a warm and spongy substance. She immediately pulled back her arm while screaming hysterically.

Her hand was now red, swollen and cold. It was also covered in a fine, powdery, dark dust. Seconds later, this same dust entered through the open window on the right side of the front of the car, and the entire family was quickly covered with it. It reportedly carried a terrible smell reminiscent of decomposing flesh.

Then, a high-pitched sound went through the vehicle — causing the family's dogs to furiously bark. The Knowles' fearful screams now became distorted — as if they were emitting sounds in slow motion. In addition, all of the hairs on their bodies stood straight up into the air.

Patrick, the oldest son, later told reporters: *"I felt like my brain was being sucked out..."*

Out of nowhere, the car was dropped back onto the pavement so abruptly that one of the tires punctured from the impact. Sean regained control of the car and hastily pulled to the side of the road. The family then scrambled out of the car and took cover in some nearby bushes. The glowing object, which was reportedly shaped like *"an egg in a cup"*, hovered around the area for a while. The horrified family felt that it was searching for them.

Finally, however, it took off at a great velocity and disappeared from view. To make sure they were safe, they decided to hide for around 30 minutes before returning to the road. They quickly changed the flat tire and raced towards the nearest sign of civilization, the Mundrabilla Roadhouse, a service station.

Much to their relief, the family managed to get there without running into the strange object again. They were greeted by several truck drivers, some of whom had witnessed a mysterious, bright light in the sky nearby. An attendant at the station later told reporters that the family were visibly wound up and frightened when they arrived.

He also inspected their vehicle and *"noticed an odor which smelled similar to hot insulation"*. In addition, Faye's hand was still swollen, and the two dogs were cowering in the car and looked to be shedding clumps of hair.

After spending some time recovering at the Roadhouse, they decided to report the terrifying event to the local police. The officers who investigated the car said that the vehicle was indeed dented, as if something had landed on it, and that it was covered in an ash-like substance.

This substance was later collected by the Victorian UFO Research Society (VUFORS) and sent to a NASA-affiliated laboratory in California, U.S. for analysis. There, Dr. Richard Haines studied the material.

Some of the dust in the car had previously been analyzed by other experts, who concluded that at least parts of it came from the interior of a burnt-out brake lining, a report which skeptics gladly accepted. Haines' closer inspection, however, resulted in a different conclusion.

The tests showed signs of oxygen, carbon, silicon, potassium, sodium chloride and strangely, a trace of astatine. Astatine is a very rare radioactive chemical element which is usually only produced via synthetic methods. Furthermore, this element should have decayed rapidly under normal circumstances, yet — when magnified — some of the particles seemed to exhibit signs of radiation.

The aftermath of the sensational event would prove to be hard for the Knowles family. They decided to leave their former home in the city of Perth, stating that most of their friends were completely taken aback by their story, thinking they had become mentally ill. Most of the locals had also been informed of their supposed meeting with alien intelligence, and many were not hesitant to ridicule them.

The Knowles also claimed that they were duped by a man named Wes Johnstone from a company named "Multi-Level Advertising", who promised to make them rich by having them appear at various promotional events.

He took their car, claiming it would serve as a marketing piece, but simply auctioned it off later to a private buyer for $7000. The family said they never saw a penny from it, and said that, in the end, the incident actually cost them around $18 000 altogether.

Being almost laughed out of their homes, grossly swindled by a con-artist and living under the constant scrutiny of skeptics, the Knowles were fed up with the whole situation. They receded back to their familiar, everyday lives and put the whole experience behind them.

Chapter 12
Peter Khoury's Intimate Encounter, 1992

Since the first reports about the paranormal phenomena were made available, a great deal of alien contact and abduction cases have been shown to have a sexual element to them. In most cases it involves some sort of professional, clinical procedure to retrieve seminal fluids from men and eggs from women.

In some other incidents, however, there are reports of more intimate relationships between the humans and the unknown beings. These accounts are often highly controversial, and much more prone to ridicule than the more common UFO reports.

Though most respectable researchers may want to leave such stories alone, there is one case in particular which, when investigated further, showed some intriguing and perplexing results. This is the story of the Australian Peter Khoury's very personal encounter.

Peter Khoury was born in Lebanon in 1964, and moved to

Australia in 1973 with his family. At school in 1981, he met his future wife, Vivian, who he married in 1990. He lived a seemingly normal life in the city of Sydney, working in the building industry and owning his own cement distribution company.

Already before the main event of this story took place, Khoury had experienced strange phenomena which altered his view of existence. In February of 1988, he and Vivian saw mysterious lights above Sydney, doing inexplicable movements while emitting a beam of light.

Later that same year, in July, while lying on the bed, he felt a sudden pressure around his ankles, as if something grabbed him. Suddenly, his entire body went numb in an instant before being completely paralyzed, yet he somehow retained ordinary waking consciousness.

He then observed three to four strange looking beings appearing around his bed. Khoury received a telepathic notion which signaled to him that he should relax and let go of his fear, stating that *"It would be like last time"*. One of the beings — a tall, thin, golden being with large black eyes — got closer to him. It looked to be preparing to insert a long, needle-like object into the top-left part of his skull. Khoury then blacked out.

After some time, Peter Khoury awoke and hastily made his way into the other room to his father and his brother, who were both in a state of deep sleep. After shaking them awake, both of them felt that only 10 minutes or so had passed since they dozed off. However, when they looked at the clock, it became obvious that well over an hour had gone by.

The next morning, Vivian discovered that there was a slight puncture mark on the side of Peter's head, surrounded by a small trace of dried blood. At this time in his life, Peter Khoury was mostly uninformed about the phenomenon of alien abduction, and he struggled to find answers to his startling and confusing experience.

Some months after the event, he came upon the book "Communion" by Whitley Stieber, by being drawn towards the cover of the book on a billboard. It showed a thin, golden, black eyed being which resembled that of his own encounter. While reading the book, he discovered that numerous characteristics of Strieber's accounts matched his own experience.

He went on to read more about UFO and ET subjects, and decided he would contact the local researchers regarding his encounter. With the more limited communication at the time, finding UFO groups and fellow experiencers proved troublesome.

The few he found also turned out to be uninterested in working with him. Frustrated by the lack of community, Khoury decided to take matters into his own hands. Later, in 1993, he founded the "UFO Experience Support Association" (UFOESA).

One year before the founding of the group, however, Peter Khoury would experience a new, even more mind-boggling event involving unknown beings. This time it would be much more intimate than the last.
On July 23rd, 1992, Khoury was lying asleep in bed at 7:30 AM. He had just driven his wife to her workplace before returning

home. He himself had been recently injured at work, and was on leave for a while. For some reason, he awoke abruptly, and was greeted with a highly-perplexing sight.

On the bed in front of him sat two, humanoid, female entities — both completely naked. The two of them had a mostly human appearance. Their bodies were fit and well proportioned, with perfectly clear skin. One of the beings closely resembled the Asian phenotype, with straight, black, medium-length hair, light brown skin and dark eyes.

The other female being had more Scandinavian features. She had light, bluish eyes and long, blonde hair. He got the impression that the blonde was communicating telepathically with the dark-haired one, giving her instructions.
Despite the many similarities to earth women, however, the females had several "alien" aspects as well. Their facial features were very sharp and chiseled. They had large cheekbones and eyes which were 2 to 3 times the normal size.

Khoury also noticed the blonde female's face in particular, which was more elongated than those of regular women. Her forehead was also quite spacious, and her hair was *"curled something like Farrah Fawcett, but to an extreme"* which *"looked really exotic in a way"*. Talking about their overall appearance, he stated: *"I have never seen a human looking like that"*.

Just having woken up moments ago, Khoury was in a groggy and highly-confused state. Before he managed to make sense of the situation, the blonde female grabbed the back of his head and pulled him close to her naked breasts. Out of fear and confusion, he resisted, which made her pull harder.

She was apparently much stronger than she looked, and planted his face against one of her nipples. For some reason unbeknownst to himself, in the heat of the moment he bit down on her nipple, and he could feel a small piece of what he presumed to be flesh getting into his mouth. The blonde female didn't recoil in pain as one might suspect she would. Instead, she calmly displayed disappointment.
Peter Khoury stated:

"The expression on her face was like "this isn't the way". In a way it was shock or confusion. She looked at the Asian one and then looked at me like, this isn't the way it's supposed to happen, you've done this wrong."

Khoury then swallowed the small piece of flesh by accident, and it got stuck in his throat. He started coughing violently, causing him to lean over the bed. When he eventually got up again, the two beings had vanished. Once he had checked the house and saw that they were gone, he went and got some water to clear his throat, but to no avail.

It would take several days before the coughing stopped completely. Later, when he went to the bathroom to urinate, he felt a painful sensation near the top of his penis. He pulled back the foreskin and discovered two thin, platinum blonde strands of hair which were tightly wrapped around it. He removed the strands and put them in a sealed plastic bag.

In 1998, author and UFO researcher, Bill Chalker, was given the hair samples to investigate. He, in turn, handed them over to a team of biochemists, who studied the strands closely using mitochondrial PCR DNA profiling. The results where perplexing.

The study showed that the strand of hair apparently belonged to someone biologically close to humans, but of an extremely rare subgroup of the Chinese Mongoloid variant.

Immediately this was seen as puzzling, as the hair sample was of a clear, blonde color as opposed to the normally dark hair of Asian people. This information was gathered from testing the shaft of the hair. When analyzing the root of the hair, however, it seemed to indicate an also extremely rare Gaelic type DNA. Back in 1998, this mixture was very confusing, but later, in the year of 2000, new discoveries in biotechnology showed that such hair transplanting with once incompatible hair could be possible while using advanced cloning techniques. Even stranger, the tests showed signs of certain genes being deleted.

More specifically, it showed two deleted genes for CCR5 protein while no intact gene for normal, undeleted CCR5 could be detected. CCR5, or C-C chemokine receptor type 5, is a protein on the surface of white blood cells which is involved in the immune system. This CCR5 deletion aspect has been known to play a part in AIDS resistance.

Based on the details of these findings, some UFO researchers have speculated that the two beings were actually human/alien hybrids, since it seemed as if someone had tinkered with their genetics.

Additionally, in "UFO lore" it is well established that many of the abduction stories related to the classic "grey" aliens and similar creatures often include some sort of genetic retrieval, in the form of harvested sperm or egg. The two beings, particularly the blonde, also had physical features which seemed to be a mix between regular humans and the very same beings which Khoury encountered in July of 1988.
In the end, the test results were staggering, but left all of the involved with more questions than answers. The physical

analysis brought a new sense of credibility to Peter Khoury's otherwise highly-controversial story, and he gained more confidence in talking about his experiences.

Peter Khoury has appeared in several documentary films since the extraordinary events took place, perhaps most notably in the 2010 production "My Mum Talks To Aliens!", by the Australian television network SBS (Special Broadcasting Service). During the documentary, he relays his story in quite some detail and shows the printed results of the biochemical tests of the hair strands. He also agreed to undergo a polygraph test, which he passed on camera.

To this day, Peter Khoury remains the head of the UFO Experience Support Association in Australia, which keeps an open door for people with similar experiences.

Chapter 13
The Ariel School Mass Sighting, 1994

The Ariel School is a private school for elementary aged children based in Ruwa, Zimbabwe which is located 12 miles from Harare, the capital of Zimbabwe.

The school was just like any other until everything changed on the 16th of September, 1994. The teachers and students of the Ariel School were just going through the motions of a normal school day when everything turned to the bizarre.

The children became bewildered with what they were witnessing. Suddenly, 5 strange objects came out of the skies. Witnesses say the objects would appear, vanish and reappear in a different spot. It was like the UFOs were playing hide and seek with the children.

Finally, one of the strange crafts — the largest one — hovered near the school and slowly landed on the hill grounds just outside the schoolyard. This was witnessed by a total of 62 students, aged 5 to 12.

One of the mothers of the children was at the school tending to her tuck shop at the time, where she was selling candies, sodas, and other snacks. The teachers of the school, meanwhile, were in a meeting when the encounter happened, and failed to get a glimpse of the fantastic incident taking place outside.

The curious children ran towards the boundary of the school to see what landed on the hills nearby. There, they saw a small figure appear on top of the craft. Some accounts of the incident say the children saw two figures and that the other one disembarked from the object and walked on the ground towards where the children were.

When the creature observed the children, it suddenly

disappeared into thin air. Moments later, it was back on its vessel. It then got inside of the craft within the blink of an eye, flew away and was never seen again. The creatures were said to be only about 3 feet tall.

The children described the strange beings as small, dark-grey men with scrawny necks, long black hair, and huge, rugby ball-like eyes. They were also apparently wearing tight, black suits.

The main creature communicated with some of the children via thoughts shared through direct eye contact before fleeing. It supposedly told them that mankind is polluting and destroying the planet and should be wise to take care of it, or else there will be dire consequences. One child in particular also recalled the alien warning them that mankind was too technologically advanced compared to its spiritual development.

Understandably, the children — especially the younger ones who were in front — were terrified. Some of them were already crying and shouting for help. The students ran to the mother who owned the tuck shop for help but she hesitated to leave her store. Others rushed to get their teachers, who thought the children were lying at first.

When the kids were dismissed for the day, they all rushed

home to tell their parents about what happened. Most of the parents went to the school right away in order to clear things up with the teachers, as many of the kids were shaken up about what had happened.

Africa's famed UFOlogist Cynthia Hind — a field investigator for MUFON — was at the scene the following day. Before arriving, she asked the headmaster, Colin Mackie, to separate the children from each other and instruct them to draw what they saw. To their amazement, all 35 drawings made that day were eerily similar. Hind then proceeded to interview 12 of the young students.

One eyewitness named Barry D. told her that he saw three objects flying in the skies with red lights flashing. He then saw the 3 craft land close to the gum trees near the school. An 11-year old girl told them about the rugby-eyes of the aliens.

Another girl said, when asked about the incident, that she swore *"by every hair on my head and the whole Bible that I am telling the truth."* When considering that children as young as they were are generally not known to lie in such an organized fashion, the fact that 62 children decided to tell the same lie seems to be quite a stretch.

It should also be noted that it wasn't the only encounter or sighting that happened during that period. A number of people say they saw UFOs flying over Zimbabwe for a couple of days before the Ariel School incident took place.

Hind documented these sightings in an article she wrote, titled "UFO Flap in Zimbabwe: Case No. 95". In it, she mentioned that a "pyrotechnic display of some magnificence" was seen by a number of people in the "almost clear night skies of this part of the continent."

She further detailed that among the witnesses were respectable people such as astronomers and scientists. Many of the witnesses also showed her sketches of the objects they saw in the sky. Almost all of them drew a zeppelin-like, yet alien-looking figure.

The late Dr. John E. Mack — then a Professor of Psychiatry from Harvard — and his associate Dominique Callimanopulos, also answered the call to investigate what happened that day in Ruwa. Mack, a Pulitzer Prize winner, conducted interviews with the children which lasted from November 28 to December 6 of the same year, with the help of Nicky Carter, a South African film producer.

Carter's half-brother worked at the school but wasn't at the premises when the encounter happened. He was later told by some of the students about the incident which led him to inform Carter, who rushed to the school and made a short documentary about the sighting. Carter strongly believes that the children were telling the truth.

Five years after the Ariel School Sighting, Mack published a book about the extraordinary event. In his book "Abduction", Mack detailed several encounters with the third kind, including the Ariel School Mass Sighting. Due to his serious attitude regarding these phenomena, his fellow academicians had their doubts regarding Mack's sanity, and he was consequently investigated by the institution.

It took a whole 14 months for Harvard to determine that there was nothing wrong with Mack and his work on UFOs. Aside from his books, Mack also lent his video recordings of his interviews with the children to the TV shows "Sightings" and "Unsolved Mysteries".

A filmmaker by the name of Randall Nickerson had also become rather fixated with the story of the Zimbabwe children and the alien beings. He, along with Callimanopulos, got permission from the John E. Mack Institute to produce a video program showing all of Mack's recorded interviews with the students. Nickerson went to Africa and spent nine months there from 2008 to 2009.

During his stay in Zimbabwe, Nickerson found other people who witnessed the same flying objects that the children saw back in 1994. Nickerson also talked to Tim Leech, the BBC reporter who went to Ruwa a few days after the encounter.

It was Leech who initially informed Mack of the sighting. Sadly, Leech died a few months after his interview with Nickerson — the only time he gave an interview regarding his experiences related to the Ruwa incident.

Nickerson, however, didn't stop there. He found many of the 62 children who witnessed the encounter. Now grown up, most of the former students had left Zimbabwe and were scattered all over the world.

When he interviewed them, what fascinated Nickerson the most was that their accounts hadn't changed at all. The stories of the children remained the same as they were back then, indicating, once again, that something truly otherworldly had made its mark that day.

Conclusion

So, after reading the accounts in this book, what are we to make of it all?

Are governments and intelligence agencies keeping information from the public?

Have beings from elsewhere already visited our planet?

One thing is for certain: Sightings of UFOs and ETs are still ongoing. With our world becoming ever more interconnected, many people are now sharing their stories between cultures and across borders.

Information that was previously only found on the fringes of society is now readily available thanks to the internet. Who knows what exciting revelations the future may bring?

Until then, keep looking up. You never know what you might see...

"The creation is vast,
Mysteries abound,
Keep the mind clear,
What is sought, shall be found."

Printed in Great Britain
by Amazon